The Herd

The Herd

Kenneth T. Williams

The Herd
first published 2023 by Scirocco Drama
An imprint of J. Gordon Shillingford Publishing Inc.
© 2023 Kenneth T. Williams

Scirocco Drama Editor: Glenda MacFarlane
Cover design by Doowah Design
Cover image based on photo of Yellowstone National Park, Lamar Valley by
Jacob W. Frank. https://www.flickr.com/photos/yellowstonenps/33942443348/.
Author photo by Aloys Fleischmann
Production photos by Nanc Price for The Citadel Theatre

Printed and bound in Canada on 100% post-consumer recycled paper.
We acknowledge the financial support of the Manitoba Arts Council and
The Canada Council for the Arts for our publishing program.

Production inquiries to the playwright at:
kennethwilliams@shaw.ca
or
feral.playwright@gmail.com

Library and Archives Canada Cataloguing in Publication

Title: The herd / Kenneth T. Williams.
Names: Williams, Kenneth T., author.
Description: A play.
Identifiers: Canadiana 20220492816 | ISBN 9781990738234 (softcover)
Classification: LCC PS8645.I4525 H47 2023 | DDC C812/.6—dc23

J. Gordon Shillingford Publishing
P.O. Box 86, RPO Corydon Avenue, Winnipeg, MB Canada R3M 3S3

I dedicate this play to Kevin Loring (AD – NAC Indigenous Theatre), for his persistence, support, and wisdom. I would not have made it without you, brother.

Photo by Aloys Fleischmann

Kenneth T. Williams

Kenneth T. Williams is a Cree playwright from the George Gordon First Nation in the Treaty 4 territory. He's the first Indigenous person to earn an MFA in Playwriting and become a professor at the University of Alberta's Department of Drama.

The Herd had a dual world premiere at the Citadel Theatre in Edmonton and Tarragon Theatre in Toronto in the summer of 2021.

Previous productions include *Gabriel Dumont's Wild West Show* (National Arts Centre), *In Care* (Gordon Tootoosis Nīkānīwin Theatre), *Café Daughter* (Gwaandak Theatre, Workshop West Playwrights Theatre, Blyth Festival), *Gordon Winter* (Persephone), *Thunderstick* (Persephone/Theatre Network), *Bannock Republic* (GTNT/Persephone), and *Three Little Birds* (Workshop West Playwrights Theatre).

He lives in Edmonton with his partner, Dr. Melissa Stoops, and their cats, Augustus and Drusilla.

Acknowledgements

First, I wish to say a massive thank you to all the stage managers I've worked with in the past and will work with in the future. Stage managers never get enough love.

This play happened because Richard Rose, then artistic director of Tarragon Theatre, shared a coffee with me in the Kensington Market in Toronto. He said, "Ken, I want you to do an Indigenous version of *An Enemy of the People.*" That's how it all started, and many thanks to him and the continuing support from Tarragon for giving me this amazing challenge.

To Daryl Cloran (AD of Citadel Theatre) and Del Surjik (former AD of Persephone Theatre), who said yes, and then had to shuffle and reshuffle their schedules as COVID wracked their seasons.

To the audiences, who are energetically (and safely) returning to our spaces to see artists on stage.

To Tara Beagan, who bravely picked up the directing mantle at the last minute.

A huge thanks to the many actors who read draft after draft and were always generous and insightful.

A special thank you to Tantoo Cardinal, who always challenges and encourages me.

A great big hug to the late Lee Maracle, who told me that I had to write this story.

To Melissa, for your love, patience, and humour.

The Canada Council for the Arts generously funded my travel to Toronto to attend the performances at Tarragon Theatre.

Foreword
By Dr. Tasha Hubbard

Ken Williams writes with what the late Danny Musqua called "the power of the pen" with equal parts courage and love to tell stories that resonate long after the curtain comes down. His plays peel back surface layers to reveal the deeper controversies and complexities facing Indigenous peoples due to the realities of living with the impacts of colonialism. Beyond the performances, Ken's work is also inherently teachable: I've taught both *Cafe Daughter* and *Gordon Winter*, and the students have found the work to be both constructive and demanding, eliciting honest discussion the way the best kinds of texts do. I look forward to teaching *The Herd* with the same result.

The Herd gives us the opportunity to reflect on how central the buffalo were and are to Plains Indigenous peoples. Most educational and historical references state that the buffalo was our main food source, and while this is accurate, it is not the full truth. Our stories and ceremonies show us that the buffalo is our relative: our grandparent who loves with benevolence, our older sibling who protects us. That relationship and its expression has been the focus of my own work for over twenty years. And ultimately, what I have come to learn is that we are in a relationship of reciprocity: we must give as much as we take.

Buffalo is our teacher. It is a keystone species, which means the buffalo hold a central role in supporting other beings with whom we share this land: the large and miniscule and everything in between. We as humans living on the Plains know we are in a reciprocal web of relationships and we are not the central character in the story of the land. Euro-western influences have sought to overturn that and foster instead a sense of individualism that relies on external gratification and recognition. Further to this, buffalo were our livelihood. We had agreements where we had responsibilities and in return, they gave themselves to us so we could survive. This is a very different concept than economy, and herein lies the central conflict of the play: how do we as Indigenous peoples navigate embracing our traditions and beliefs in a capitalist society that demands both dollars and views?

The buffalo's targeted destruction to clear the path for capitalism cut us deeply. Plains Indigenous peoples are all recovering from their near-loss, and finding our way back from this and other waves of genocide is messy, beautiful, difficult. As the academy reminds us, settler colonialism is not a historic event, it's also now. Indigenous lands have been taken and our livelihoods destroyed in ongoing projects of constant consumption and replacement.

And as *The Herd* reminds us, even our very identities as Indigenous peoples are seen as fair game. There has been the recent exposure of people who claim to be Indigenous but have no lived experience and only a distant ancestor from hundreds of years ago. While there must always be room for people who have been displaced in more recent times to find their way back, such as those affected by the now notorious '60s scoop, this is something entirely different. And those who do take on an Indigenous identity so often grab the microphone and step on a soapbox and proclaim they represent Indigenous peoples and our struggle.

The Herd also grapples with thorny subjects like purity, gene technology, and authenticity. It pushes us to think about what really matters when two white buffalo calves are born. In the end, how people choose to live and enter into a future that truly embraces what those calves represent is what matters. As Vanessa says, "When you are home, I know I am home," and this echoes how many Indigenous peoples feel as we welcome the buffalo home to reserve lands in increasing numbers. The future includes buffalo and we as humans need to give them the space they deserve to decide for themselves, to be the sovereign beings they are born to be.

Dr. Tasha Hubbard (Cree) is a filmmaker and an associate professor in the Faculty of Native Studies and the Department of English and Film at the University of Alberta. She is from Peepeekisis First Nation in Treaty Four Territory and has direct ties to Thunderchild First Nation in Treaty Six Territory. She is also the mother of a sixteen-year-old son. She is a multiple-award-winning filmmaker. She researches and champions Indigenous efforts to restore the buffalo, has been a supporter of the Buffalo Treaty since 2015, and is a founding board member of the International Buffalo Relations Institute. Her latest feature documentary in progress is called Singing Back the Buffalo.

Men standing with pile of buffalo skulls, Michigan Carbon Works, Rougeville MI, 1892. (Burton Historical Collection, Detroit Public Library)

View of a pile of stacked buffalo skulls, a man is standing in front, either in Medicine Hat in 1884 or Saskatoon in 1890. (Provincial Archives of Alberta)

Production History

The Herd was co-commissioned by Tarragon Theatre (Toronto) and Persephone Theatre (Saskatoon) and premiered in a co-production of The Citadel Theatre (Edmonton, April 9, 2022) and Tarragon Theatre (Toronto, May 18, 2022), in association with the National Arts Centre Indigenous Theatre.

Cast

Tai Amy Grauman	Vanessa Brokenhorn
Todd Houseman	Coyote Jackson
Cheyenne Scott	Aislinn Kennedy
Sharon Shorty / Shyanne Duquette	Sheila Kennedy
Dylan Thomas-Bouchier	Michael "Baby Pete" Brokenhorn

Creative Team

Tara Beagan	Director
Shyanne Duquette	Apprentice Director
Andy Moro	Set & Video Designer
Peter Spike Lyne	Lighting Designer
Hailey Verbonac	Assistant LX & Video Designer
Samantha McCue	Costume Designer
Mishelle Cuttler	Sound Designer
Sang Sang Lee	Stage Manager
Yvette Martens	Assistant Stage Manager

Aislinn (Cheyenne Scott) explains to Baby Pete (Dylan Thomas-Bouchier) that she's heard about the buffalo calves in Ireland and decided to visit Vanessa's lab. Photo by Nanc Price for The Citadel Theatre (2022).

Aislinn (Cheyenne Scott) pours tea for Aunt Sheila (Shyanne Duquette) as they play Radio Bingo. Photo by Nanc Price for The Citadel Theatre (2022).

Aunt Sheila (Shyanne Duquette) in shadow, about to reveal her buffalo calf sculptures. Photo by Nanc Price for The Citadel Theatre (2022).

The cast as the buffalo herd. Photo by Nanc Price for The Citadel Theatre (2022).

Vanessa (Tai Amy Grauman) in her lab. Photo by Nanc Price for The Citadel Theatre (2022).

Baby Pete (Dylan Thomas-Bouchier) invites Coyote (Todd Houseman) to visit his reserve to see the calves for himself. Photo by Nanc Price for The Citadel Theatre (2022).

Coyote (Todd Houseman) "Indigenizing" the internet as he updates his followers on his travels to the Buffalo Pound Lake First Nation. Photo by Nanc Price for The Citadel Theatre (2022).

Vanessa (Tai Amy Grauman) grills Coyote (Todd Houseman) over his real reasons for coming to the reserve. Photo by Nanc Price for The Citadel Theatre (2022).

Coyote (Todd Houseman) wrapped in a buffalo robe. Photo by Nanc Price for The Citadel Theatre (2022).

Cast of *The Herd*. Photo by Nanc Price for The Citadel Theatre, (2022).

Characters

MICHAEL "BABY PETE" BROKENHORN: Cree/Dakota, 30ish, Chief of Pitokahan Sakahikan (Buffalo Pound Lake First Nation). Vanessa's older brother. Wears a Saskatchewan Roughriders jersey with Baby Pete written on it. This actor will also play DOUBTER, NDN FOLLOWER, EAGER DONOR, and COLIN'S COUSIN.

SHEILA KENNEDY: Cree, 50s, is considered an elder but doesn't want to be. A sculptor who works in clay. Vanessa and Baby Pete's aunt. She often talks to her dead sister. This actor will also play NEW AGE BOOKSTORE OWNER, MIRACLE DONOR, and PISSED-OFF ELDER.

AISLINN KENNEDY: 30ish, Irish, a representative of the European Union. Dublin born and raised. Not a country person. This actor will also play COMPUTER VOICE, PSYCHIC BELIEVER, DONOR, COLIN'S CLASSMATE, and TOTAL NEWBIE.

COYOTE JACKSON: looks Indigenous, late/mid-30s, editor and main writer of Red Warrior Media, a web-based news site. He dresses like he's going to a protest, and he always—ALWAYS—wears combat pants. He almost always has a cell phone or small tablet connected to a high-end selfie stick with a swivel mount. This actor will also play RADIO BINGO CALLER.

VANESSA BROKENHORN: Cree/Dakota, 30ish but looks younger, veterinarian for the Pitokahan Sakahikan's bison herd. Vanessa always dresses to work with the bison. Her clothes must be comfortable, something that you would expect could deal with blood, shit, spit and mud. When indoors, she puts on a white lab coat.

Setting

Various locations around the Pitokahan Sakahikan First Nation (AKA Buffalo Pound Lake First Nation) located in the Qu'Appelle Valley, the Treaty 4 Territory in Saskatchewan.

Vanessa's lab in the West Range. Buffalo Paddock. Sheila's house. Baby Pete's office. Gate to the north range.

There is the suggestion of a giant buffalo on stage. It is hidden as much as it is integral. It is as essential to the set as the buffalo were essential to the Peoples of the Plains. It can appear and disappear with lighting. It is evasive, wary. You may catch a glimpse of it from the corner of your eye but it's difficult to see if you try to look right at it. It can easily vanish in a heartbeat or a gunshot.

Keep set changes to a minimum. If something is on stage, it should be useful for as many scenes as possible.

Action flows from scene to scene. No blackouts preferred.

Time: Now-ish, the early summer, after the calving season.

Disclaimer: This is a work of fiction. Names, characters, businesses, places, events, locales, and incidents are either the products of the playwright's imagination or used in a fictitious manner. Any resemblance to actual persons, living or dead, or actual events is purely coincidental.

Notes on the Text

— means the speaker suddenly stops or is interrupted.

… means a trail-off.

/ means the next character starts their line.

Pauses are active, they are to be treated as silent battles of wills between characters. The first to speak, loses.

Aislinn is pronounced "Ash-LEEN," Siobhan is pronounced "Sheh-VAUN," and Roisin is pronounced "ROY-sheen." Slough is pronounced the Western Canadian way, "slew."

SFX: We hear a large bison herd rumble by. The ground should shake. The bison huff and chuff as they run by.

SFX: Gunshots. Lots and lots of gunshots until we feel we are in a war zone.

PROJECTION: A bison skull, stark white against the blackness. Then another, and another, until we see a mountain of skulls, overwhelmingly huge and overpowering.

Red drips and flows over the scene.

We see BABY PETE and SHEILA, as bison, emerge in redness.

BABY PETE: It begins with the apocalypse.

SHEILA: We roamed here.

We see AISLINN, as a bison.

AISLINN: "Kill every buffalo you can!"

SHEILA: And we were slaughtered.

AISLINN: "For every buffalo dead is an Indian gone."

BABY PETE: For fertilizer.

SHEILA: For the plates on your table.

AISLINN: Enemies.

BABY PETE: For the land.

SHEILA: For the land.

AISLINN:	Refugees.
SHEILA:	But there is hope.
BABY PETE:	Hope.
SHEILA:	A prophecy.

We see COYOTE, as a bison.

COYOTE:	A prophecy.
BABY PETE:	We will return.
COYOTE:	And when you do?
BABY PETE:	We have returned.
COYOTE:	And now what?
AISLINN:	Not millions.
COYOTE:	How many then?
SHEILA:	Not thousands.
COYOTE:	What's going to happen?
BABY PETE:	But enough.

SFX: The grunts, snuffling, and pawing of bison, much fewer than before.

We see VANESSA.

SHEILA:	She moves easily among us.
BABY PETE:	She's the only one we trust.
VANESSA:	You are the most beautiful creatures in the world. When you are home, I know I am home.

A *moment of tranquility...*

SFX: Cell phone rings.

The bison scatter.

She looks at her phone.

VANESSA: People, on the other hand.

COYOTE holding the phone to his ear.

SFX: Cell phone ringing, followed by...

VANESSA: *(Into her phone.)* This is Dr. Brokenhorn. I don't answer calls from numbers I don't recognize. *(Electronic.)Beeeeep!*

COYOTE: *(Into phone.)* Hi, Vanessa, I mean Dr. Brokenhorn. This is Coyote Jackson. I'm a blogger with—

VANESSA: *(Electronic.) Beeeeeeeeep.* Mailbox is full.

She hangs up.

COYOTE: Huh?... Ooookay.

SHEILA is working on a clay buffalo sculpture, talking to her dead sister, SIOBHAN.

SHEILA: We know prophecies come true. Sometimes more than once. Like the apocalypse. A priest in the residential school was teaching us about the apocalypse in the bible to scare us into wanting to be Christians. Well me, being the smart mouth I was, said "We had ours already." And he said, "what do you mean you had yours already? It hasn't happened." No sir, it happened. Death, pestilence, war, false gods. That all happened when the white man showed up. By my calculation, we're about halfway through it.

Pause.

Got strapped good for that one.

Pause.

Was worth it, though, to see his face.

She examines her buffalo.

She's not happy with it and mashes the clay together to start again.

SHEILA: I don't know, I just don't know why this is causing so much trouble. Something is blocking me.

BABY PETE is on the phone talking to COYOTE.

BABY PETE: We just got our land claim settlement when I ran for chief. I said, look, we can spend our money on a new water system but then that money is gone. And we'll have to come up with more money to maintain it that we just do not have. We have an aquifer right beneath us, but we can't drink it because we have no way to get it out of the ground. You know what I mean?

COYOTE: Yes—well, not really—I've never lived on a—

BABY PETE: The water we do have, it's not drinkable. We've been boiling it for nearly twenty years.

COYOTE: That's horrible and all but what about—

BABY PETE: But, we kinda got used to it so I said, "After we get the herd, we'll use the profits to buy and maintain our own water system from the aquifer." We keep talking about buffalo as something from the past. I said, "The buffalo can be our future again. We can buy extra land with the settlement and get a commercial herd."

COYOTE: And the white ones?

BABY PETE: That's why I want you to come here, man! See them for yourself. Experience this up close and personal.

COYOTE: Your sister—I mean, Dr. Brokenhorn—she'll talk to me?

BABY PETE: She has to. I'm the chief. I'm the one who made the deal.

COYOTE: Well, if you think that's okay.

BABY PETE: When can you get here?

COYOTE: I'm not far.

BABY PETE: Text or call me when you get here. Peace out.

                BABY PETE hangs up.

                COYOTE sets the phone into his selfie stick. He's doing what the media call a "stand up" with it.

COYOTE: *(Into phone camera.)* Aniin and Boozhoo, faithful Red Media Warriors. 'Tis I, Coyote Jackson, Indigenizer of the Internet. Here's our good medicine for the week. I'm on the Buffalo Pound Lake First Nation in the Treaty 4 Territory—that's Saskatchewan for you settler folk. You saw them photos on the forum, right? Not one, but two—count 'em, two!—two white buffalo calves were born right here, last week! Are they for real? Is this the prophecy coming true? I'll be in the middle, updating you on the regular, making sure you get it first and fast, here on Red Warrior Media. Aho!

                He clicks off then his phone beeps.

COMPUTER
VOICE: *(Electronic.)* You have one video message.

He swipes his phone to hear the message.

DOUBTER: *(Aggressive.)* "Coyote" Jackson? You are so full of shit! More like COLIN JACKSON from Etobicoke. ETOBICOKE! Here's his photo from his Grade 7—

COYOTE kills the video.

COMPUTER
VOICE: *(Electronic.)* Do you wish to upload video to website?

COYOTE swipes a button.

COMPUTER
VOICE: *(Electronic.)* Video deleted.

VANESSA in her lab.

SFX: Her cell phone rings... and rings... and rings.

She declines the call.

AISLINN enters.

A cold moment between them.

VANESSA: I wasn't expecting—what are you doing here?

AISLINN: It's like I never left. You're wearing the same clothes. You still keep your hair tucked up and away. I told you, let it fall naturally. You're lucky. It just lays out beautifully on its own. I'm not so lucky as you.

VANESSA keeps her distance.

VANESSA: Still wondering why you're here.

AISLINN: The twins. Of course.

VANESSA: Probably a bovine gene.

AISLINN:	Probably?
VANESSA:	Makes the most sense.
AISLINN:	When will you be sure?
VANESSA:	What's the hurry?
AISLINN:	Just doing my due diligence for the European Union. We are partners, remember?
VANESSA:	Diligence, bordering on harassment.
AISLINN:	"Harassing" you! I am not harassing you. I'm concerned because you didn't tell me about the calves.
VANESSA:	Like I said, could be a bovine gene. So more than likely nothing to get worked up about.
AISLINN:	You should've told me right away.
VANESSA:	Didn't see the need.
AISLINN:	Exactly why I'm here. You don't see the need to keep your partners informed of a major development.
VANESSA:	This isn't a development—
AISLINN:	It is so a "development." One that has massive implications for our project. You know what I mean. This will cause excitement.
VANESSA:	That's why we must keep it a secret.
AISLINN:	Too late for that. I heard about it. In Ireland. Bison suppliers there are buzzing. They see the marketing opportunities and they'll want to know if we're talking about the real deal or not.
VANESSA:	It could a year before we know for sure what caused their white fur.

AISLINN:	Stop bluffing me. I've already talked to the University of Saskatchewan and I know they're running those DNA scans, or whatever you call them, right now. They're pretty sure we'll know in a week or two.
VANESSA:	You still could've done all this from Dublin.
AISLINN:	But I love coming here this time of year. The weather is wonderfully pleasant. And no crowds. I may spend a couple of days at Katepwa Beach. If it's not too windy.
VANESSA:	You? Hanging around with the "peasants" at the beach?
AISLINN:	They have their charms.
VANESSA:	Witches have charms.
AISLINN:	Ooooh, so you're not letting that go. He's forgiven me. Why can't you?
VANESSA:	Why should I?
AISLINN:	He seems fine now.
VANESSA:	And he is.
AISLINN:	So what's the problem?
VANESSA:	If you can do that to him, you can do it to me.
AISLINN:	I am flattered, Vanessa, I really am but you're not—
VANESSA:	Get over yourself! I'm talking about the research. I'm talking about the herd.
AISLINN:	You are so paranoid.
VANESSA:	Don't fuck with my girls.

BABY PETE enters.

He's surprised to see AISLINN.

BABY PETE: Aislinn!

AISLINN: Michael.

Pause.

BABY PETE: It's great to see you again.

AISLINN: And you as well. Is your Aunt Sheila still at the same place?

They move to hug then realize it wouldn't be a good idea.

BABY PETE: So, you were just in the neighbourhood?

AISLINN: We do have the internet, you know. Makes it harder to keep secrets.

BABY PETE: I hear ya. We have a blogger coming.

VANESSA: A blogger! What blogger?

AISLINN: Just a blogger? I thought this would've attracted more attention.

VANESSA: I don't want more attention.

AISLINN: Well. He'll have to do. For now. He presents a great opportunity to publicize the arrangement you have with the EU.

BABY PETE: I'm pretty sure he's not here about the arrangement.

AISLINN: Of course he's not. So, while we wait for the results, punch up the arrangement. Gives him something to blog about. For now.

VANESSA: Here five minutes and she's bossing you around. Just like old times.

BABY PETE: Sis, give it a rest.

VANESSA: No. Not after what she did—

BABY PETE: Vanessa!

>   *COYOTE enters. Stops. Looks around.*

>   *Pause.*

COYOTE: Hi. I'm—

BABY PETE: You're Coyote Jackson!

COYOTE: Yes, I'm looking for—

BABY PETE: You freakin' made it!

>   *BABY PETE bear hugs COYOTE.*

BABY PETE: I am so glad you're here.

COYOTE: Me too.

BABY PETE: I'm such a big fan of your work.

COYOTE: Thanks.

>   *BABY PETE finally releases him.*

BABY PETE: Big fan.

COYOTE: Really appreciate that.

BABY PETE: So glad you're here. Man!

COYOTE: I really would like to speak to Dr. Brokenhorn.

BABY PETE: Yes, of course! Where are my manners?

>   *He stands aside, indicating VANESSA. She glares at him. A silent game of head nods and hand gestures between the siblings escalates to where BABY PETE manhandles VANESSA towards COYOTE.*
>
>   *If glares were daggers, the lab would be covered in BABY PETE's blood.*

Pause.

AISLINN hands COYOTE her card.

AISLINN: *(To COYOTE.)* My name is Aislinn Kennedy, I represent the European Union. We're partners with the Buffalo Pound Lake First Nation. We've invested in their bison operation as well as the research Dr. Brokenhorn is doing with genetic cataloguing and purification of the herd.

COYOTE: Okay, thank you. That's interesting and all, but I'm more focused on the white calves that were just born.

AISLINN: Yes, I'm sure, just know that we fully support Dr. Brokenhorn. Her research. And the First Nation. Fully. If you have any background questions, just call me.

COYOTE: Thank you. I will.

Pause.

BABY PETE looks at his phone.

BABY PETE: Oh hey, I gotta go. Aunt Sheila wants me to pick up her cards at the gas station for Radio Bingo.

AISLINN: Radio Bingo! I forgot how much I loved Radio Bingo.

BABY PETE: Well, come on over!

BABY PETE and AISLINN exit.

Pause.

COYOTE: Well...I'd like to start the—

VANESSA silences him with a raised finger.

She circles him, examining him.

This makes COYOTE uneasy and he applies some aromatherapy balm to his wrists, temples, back of his neck, and behind each ear.

VANESSA sniffs and is repelled.

VANESSA: What is that?

COYOTE: It's called "Sacred Sage."

VANESSA: "Sacred Sage?"

COYOTE: You can have some if you like.

He offers the balm, but she declines.

VANESSA: Your outfit. Very Oka, 1990.

COYOTE: Yeah, well, it was an inspiring time for our people.

VANESSA: You Mohawk?

COYOTE: No. No. I meant. I mean, our people as in Indigenous people. *(Indicating his equipment.)* Do you mind if I start recording?

VANESSA: Haven't decided, yet.

COYOTE: Okay.

VANESSA: You look kind of young to have been at Oka.

COYOTE: I wasn't there. I just read about it.

VANESSA: Hey. Me too.

COYOTE: But man, I wish I was.

VANESSA: As what? A warrior? Or reporter?

COYOTE: Both! When I saw those images of the army laying out the razor wire and pointing their rifles at our women, it just—*uuuuggh!*—enraged me, you know.

VANESSA: So, that kind of conflict excites you?

COYOTE: Oh! Yeah, totally. This is different, though. A happy story. Exciting too.

VANESSA: What do you know about this, anyway?

COYOTE: Well. It's not every day a prophecy is fulfilled. Twin white calves? That's got to be the sign.

VANESSA: And if you want to talk about the prophecy, you'll need to talk to an Elder. One that knows about this in particular. I won't talk about the prophecy.

COYOTE: But you know about it?

VANESSA: Of course I know about it. You grow up here, you definitely know about it. But that's not what you really want to know, is it?

COYOTE: Well, I was going to get around to—

VANESSA: You want to know if I "made them" on purpose?

            SHEILA in her home, working on the sculpture.

SHEILA: I saw this photo, today, on the internet. It was of two buffalo, made of clay, in a cave in Europe somewhere. France, I think. They believe the sculpture is fifteen thousand years old or something. Remarkable. The detail. You can see where the artist's fingernails scraped the clay.

            She works the clay.

We are buffalo people. The Cree and Dakota. And you could tell they were buffalo people. Whoever made that sculpture, I mean. They're in a cave, so the only light would be fire. A fire flickering on them would, I don't know, make them look like they're running or something.

Hums a traditional song.

What songs did they sing when they visited that cave? What were the stories they shared? How did their voices sound, echoing in that cave?

Humming, improvising, traditional-sounding, then a shock.

I can't do this. It's too much, I can't do this!

Covers the sculpture.

I can't do this.

BABY PETE: *(Offstage, yelling.)* Aunty! Guess who's come for a visit?

SHEILA composes herself.

AISLINN and BABY PETE enter.

SHEILA: Aislinn! So nice to see you!

A genuine hug between them.

Aislinn produces a box of Brady's Irish Tea.

SHEILA: Brady's tea! Ooooooh! Thank you. We didn't expect to see you so soon.

AISLINN: It's great to see you too, Sheila.

BABY PETE: Your cards.

*BABY PETE and SHEILA perform a good
luck "ritual" when they exchange the cards.*

SHEILA: Thank you, nephew. *(To Aislinn.)* Have you seen Vanessa yet?

AISLINN: Briefly. She's still...you know.

SHEILA: Oh, don't worry. I'm sure you two will patch things up.

AISLINN: With her memory? It would take a miracle.

SHEILA: We've had one with the calves, so anything's possible. Did you get your cards for Radio Bingo?

AISLINN: Of course!

BABY PETE: *(Re: the covered sculpture.)* Is that for the Elders Lodge?

SHEILA: No. Not yet, it isn't.

Back to COYOTE and VANESSA.

COYOTE: Well. Yes. Of course. I know you're also a geneticist. You're "purifying" the herd. So, I have to know if you're using genetic modification or not.

VANESSA: We are using bison genes. Just bison genes. We are, in reality, de-modifying what was... well, not modified but mixed. What I'm trying to do is make the bison more like their ancestors when they met my ancestors. Those two girls out there, we don't know if their white fur is from a bison or bovine gene.

COYOTE: But if they're mostly buffalo, wouldn't that mean it's more than likely a buffalo gene?

VANESSA: No. In fact, I'd bet that it's a bovine gene. They're snowy white. If it was the typical bison gene causing the whiteness, they'd be turning redder by now. And since I'm not positive why they're white, all talk of prophecy and whatever should be kept quiet.

COYOTE: But don't you want people to know about them?

VANESSA: No, definitely not. My community is relying on the health of this herd, and anything that upsets them or my research could cost us—

> *SFX: Drums, not powwow drums, just drums, in the distance, outside.*

VANESSA: You hear that?

> *VANESSA's phone rings. She looks at the number then answers it.*

VANESSA: What's going on, Michael?

BABY PETE: It's like some kind of parade.

> *SFX: Bad powwow drumming and singing.*

VANESSA: Parade?

COYOTE: Oh. They must be here already.

VANESSA: Coyote seems to know something about this.

> *She stands outside to see what the noise is about.*

VANESSA: Michael, there must be a hundred people out there. They're heading for the west range! *(To COYOTE.)* What do you know about this?

COYOTE: When I told my subscribers I was coming out here, a bunch said it would be a good idea.

VANESSA: There's like a hundred people out there and they're heading towards the bison.

COYOTE: They want to see the calves.

VANESSA: They can't see the calves! Get them away from there. *(To BABY PETE.)* These are Coyote's people.

COYOTE: They're not my—

VANESSA shushes him with her hand.

VANESSA: I'm heading into the herd to move them away a bit. *(She disconnects.)* Find my brother and keep these lunatics away from my girls.

He's taking selfies.

VANESSA: Don't stand there gawking! Move!

She grabs his jacket and marches him out.

VANESSA, with gestures and calls, moves the herd.

BABY PETE and COYOTE watch Vanessa.

SFX: Drums from before, a little closer.

COYOTE: She's like a buffalo whisperer.

BABY PETE: Don't, I beg you, don't ever, ever call her that. To her face.

COYOTE: I'm amazed they found you guys so fast. I got lost on the way here.

BABY PETE: Let me guess, you found a town called—

COYOTE: Called Buffalo Pound Lake. Yeah. It made sense that you'd be there. But everyone laughed when I asked about the reserve.

BABY PETE: We were supposed to be there when our chief was told to pick a reserve. But the land was "too good" for Indians so the government shifted us here to be "near our own kind." We kept the name as a reminder of where we're supposed to be. Wait a second. How many more are planning on coming?

COYOTE looks at his tablet.

COYOTE: Not sure, really, but the threads are blowing up. Like, wow, really blowing... *(Glances at his tablet.)* I wasn't the only one who made the mistake about the location. Looks like a few hundred people ended up at the real Buffalo Pound Lake.

COYOTE types furiously.

BABY PETE: A few hundred?

COYOTE: I guess there aren't enough hotels or camp sites.

COYOTE keeps typing furiously.

BABY PETE: What are you writing?

COYOTE: Just letting everyone know that the reserve isn't near the lake.

BABY PETE: Just tell them to stay away.

COYOTE: I'll suggest—

BABY PETE: At least get those people away from the fences! For their own safety.

COYOTE: On it.

BABY PETE approaches VANESSA.

VANESSA:	I need riders out there. As soon as possible. Maybe they can lead the herd into the valley. Away from those crazies.
BABY PETE:	Will do.
VANESSA:	And get Coyote off the reserve. He's barely here an hour and look at the chaos he's created.

AISLINN and SHEILA have their bingo cards out.

AISLINN:	B-15, come on, B-15.
RADIO BINGO CALLER:	And the next number up is...
AISLINN:	B-15!
RADIO BINGO CALLER:	O-70/Oh-seven-zero
AISLINN:	Boris Johnson's bollocks!
SHEILA:	Maybe we should switch to caffeine-free tea.
RADIO BINGO CALLER:	We're going to put Radio Bingo on hold. I know you all probably need a pee break right now. I certainly do!

SFX: Classic rock plays through the radio.

AISLINN:	I could use something stronger.
SHEILA:	I don't have anything stronger, I'm afraid. Where are you staying while you're here?
AISLINN:	I have a cabin at the Beach.
SHEILA:	Nonsense. You're staying with me.

AISLINN: That's very generous, but doesn't...

SHEILA: She practically lives out in her lab now. You won't run into each other here.

AISLINN: Well, thank you. It won't be long. I'm just here for an update.

SHEILA: Just an "update"?

AISLINN: All right, all right. I had to see them too. With my own eyes.

SHEILA: They have many people worked up around here.

AISLINN: What do you think about the calves? I know they're supposed to be a sign of something. A prophecy.

SHEILA: Yes. But I don't know it very well. My sister, Siobhan, knew it better than I did. She was supposed to be the "Elder" in our family.

AISLINN: Siobhan? Your sister's name was Siobhan?

SHEILA: Yes.

AISLINN: I have a sister named Siobhan. Maybe we're long-lost relatives.

SHEILA: Well, that would depend if you have bootleggers in your family.

AISLINN: If I looked hard enough, I'd probably find me one or two.

SHEILA: Joe Kennedy was his name. An American bootlegger who fell in love with my grandmother. She ran away to the big city of Moose Jaw and worked as a waitress. This was during Prohibition. She made really good money, she said, because the bootleggers liked to tip. And the biggest tipper was this American fella with the nice teeth. He took a liking to her. She took a liking to him. They had a baby. My dad. My grandmother said Joe was super happy. He wrote her often. Sent money.

Pause.

AISLINN: And?

SHEILA: He was a bootlegger, you know. Probably got killed or just moved on.

AISLINN: Still. A brigand with good teeth. The rogue's charm.

SHEILA: Oh, I don't know if I believe any of it. Who knows how much is really true.

SFX: Classic rock in the back fades out.

RADIO BINGO
CALLER: And we're back! Big news out on the highway. We got a bunch of tourists wanting to look at the white buffalo. Baby Pete just called me and is requesting that the people who worked powwow security give him a hand out there. He says he'll be by the West Range where the crowd is gathering. I guess it's hard to miss. Okay, back to the game.

AISLINN: I better get to the lab.

SHEILA: I'll come with. Sounds exciting.

RADIO BINGO
CALLER: And the next number is? O-15.

AISLINN: Bollocks!

                                    COYOTE with BABY PETE. He's got the
                                    selfie stick up and recording. BABY PETE
                                    is trying to teach COYOTE how to properly
                                    pronounce "Buffalo Pound Lake in Cree."

BABY PETE: *Pee-toh—*

COYOTE: *Pee-toh...*

BABY PETE: Pee-toh-cahan.

COYOTE: Pin-to-can?

BABY PETE: *Pee-toh-cahan Sah-kah-Hee-gahn.*

COYOTE: *Sa-ga—*

BABY PETE: *Sah-kah-Hee-*

COYOTE: Okay, okay, I got it. *(Into the tablet.)* Aniin
                        Warriors. 'Tis I, Coyote Jackson, coming to
                        you from the Pinto-Sockey-Van.

BABY PETE: Pee-toh-cahan—

COYOTE: Buffalo Pound Lake First Nation. I'm with
                        the chief, Michael Brokenhorn, and we'd both
                        like to—

BABY PETE: Baby Pete.

COYOTE: Excuse me?

BABY PETE: Baby Pete. No one calls me Michael. Except
                        my sister and my aunt.

COYOTE: Why's that?

BABY PETE: Just a rez nickname. Don't you have one?

COYOTE:	Uh. No. I don't. I wasn't raised on a reserve.
BABY PETE:	No? Okay. I won't hold it against you.
COYOTE:	Thanks?
BABY PETE:	Anyway. I'm the chief of Pihtokahan—
COYOTE:	*(Interrupting.)* Pihtokahan Sakahikan—
BABY PETE:	Yes. Correct. And we're a small reserve. We don't have any extra housing or anything, we don't have any drinkable water, and we'd like it if you didn't all come down here. All at once, I mean. We have no means of taking care of so many visitors. If you all just stayed home, we'd greatly appreciate it. We'll send you plenty of photographs and video if you like but, like I said, there's no place for you all to stay.
COYOTE:	Thank you, chief. I can vouch for how small this reserve is.
BABY PETE:	We're using most of our land for the buffalo herd. So we're kind of cramped. And, we don't want anybody, you know, harming our beautiful girls here. They're very special to us.
COYOTE:	They're here because they want to show their respect to them. They wouldn't harm them one bit. *(To camera.)* Am I right, warriors? Am I right!
BABY PETE:	Yeah, yeah, that's fine. We don't want to get the buffalo too excited.
COYOTE:	Can I get an "aho," chief?
	Pause.
BABY PETE:	*(Anything to end this awkward moment.)* Ahaw.

> *COYOTE belts out a high-pitched war whoop.*

COYOTE: *(To camera.)* There you have it, warriors! Please, respect these people and their sacred lands and keep your distance.

> *He clicks off his tablet.*

BABY PETE: You think that'll help?

COYOTE: Honestly? I can't keep up with the forums and threads and sub-threads. People are going nuts over this.

> *VANESSA enters.*

VANESSA: Why is he still here?

BABY PETE: We just did an announcement. His people will stay away.

VANESSA: They're right over there! Having all these people around will stress them out. Michael, I know what's best for the herd. Send these people away.

> *AISLINN and SHEILA enter.*

SHEILA: Wow, that's quite a crowd.

AISLINN: Who are they? Where are they from?

VANESSA: *(To AISLINN.)* What are you doing out here?

AISLINN: Well, you didn't just expect me to turn around and leave, did you?

VANESSA: I mean, out here in the range. All of you, please leave! There's enough people out here as it is.

SHEILA: Now, Vanessa. We're here to help.

VANESSA:	Then march this jackass to the fence and get him to clear his people out of here.
COYOTE:	They're NOT my people.

AISLINN and SHEILA march COYOTE to the fence.

COYOTE:	*(To SHEILA.)* Excuse me, are you an Elder?
SHEILA:	No, do I look "elderly" enough?
COYOTE:	No. Well, maybe a little bit.
SHEILA:	*Mee-sis!(Cree slang for "you little shit.")*
AISLINN:	This is Sheila Kennedy. Michael and Vanessa's aunt. Sheila, this is Coyote. A blogger of some kind.
SHEILA:	Blogger?
COYOTE:	I've been posting on the white buffalo.
AISLINN:	And mentioning the EU's arrangement?
COYOTE:	Haven't had the chance.
AISLINN:	We're the main financial partner to the First Nation and—
COYOTE:	*(To SHEILA.)* I'm sorry I mistook you for an Elder.
SHEILA:	That's quite all right. I'm not that offended.
AISLINN:	You're only saying that because he's cute.

BABY PETE and VANESSA in her lab.

BABY PETE:	What's got you so worked up?
VANESSA:	You have to ask?
BABY PETE:	Aislinn and I worked it out. It's all in the past.

VANESSA: That look you gave her wasn't in the past.

BABY PETE: That was not—no—I was caught off guard. I didn't expect to see her so soon.

VANESSA: I'm sure the European Union could spare someone else to do the spying for them.

BABY PETE: It's her project.

VANESSA: It's my project.

BABY PETE: It was Aislinn who sold the proposal to the EU. We couldn't have done it without her. Which you agreed to.

VANESSA: That was before...you guys.

BABY PETE: Hey, we were both adults and...it didn't work out.

VANESSA: That's why you're handling it so well. You've suppressed all the shitty things she did to you.

BABY PETE: It wasn't that bad.

VANESSA: Yes, it was, Michael. I can still see Aunty's face when you called her. Her driving through the night like a maniac. Seeing you at the slough where Mom and Dad died. None of that goes away for me. I don't have the luxury of forgetting, like you do. I never have. If it wasn't for the herd, for those girls...

BABY PETE: C'mon, sis, don't say that.

VANESSA: I'm just saying if she can do that in her personal life, to someone she considers a business partner and a friend, then... Just remember your promise to me, to this community, and to the herd. Especially, to the herd.

AISLINN, SHEILA and COYOTE at the fence.

SFX: Drums and singing in the distance.

SHEILA: Those people don't really think that's how you dance powwow, do they?

AISLINN: *(To COYOTE.)* Where are you from, again?

COYOTE: From the None-of-your-damn-business Indigenous Nation.

AISLINN: Don't take offence. I'm sure everyone here has asked you the same question.

COYOTE: That's between us Native people. That's not a question for white-colonizer-settler-tards.

AISLINN: Why, aren't you a master with words.

COYOTE: You just don't go off asking questions like that.

AISLINN: Funny you say that, because people are talking about a...*(Looks at her tablet.)* Colin Jackson, from...*(Pronounces it wrong.)* Etobicoke, Ontario.

SHEILA: Who's this Colin Jackson?

AISLINN: There are threads and threads about how you're some white boy from the suburbs of Toronto.

SHEILA: Him?

SHEILA looks him over.

AISLINN: It's all over his blog.

She hands SHEILA her tablet so she can look.

COYOTE: *(To himself.)* I need a new admin. *(To SHEILA.)* Don't pay attention to those comments.

SHEILA: *(To AISLINN.)* So, you just decided to snoop on him.

AISLINN: I was just checking his blog. For updates, postings about the herd. And these threads are hard to miss.

COYOTE: What can I say? The world is full of haters.

AISLINN: There's even a photo from your high school yearbook that looks remarkably like you.

COYOTE: That person doesn't exist anymore.

AISLINN: I believe that person is standing right in front of me. What do you call them, Sheila, "pretendians"?

COYOTE: I'm not a pretendian, or whatever. That was me. Before I found out. My family had a "secret" history. One that they were ashamed of.

AISLINN: Indian princess in the family tree?

SHEILA: Aislinn, don't be mean.

COYOTE: No, not like that. We're not Cherokee. I'm a descendant of a country wife. On my mother's side. Probably Algonquin or Huron.

AISLINN: A country wife? What was her name?

COYOTE: Not recorded.

AISLINN: Then how do you know?

COYOTE: We have my mother's family tree, going back to the early 1700s. And Honore-Joseph Archambault is listed as the father of an "enfant sauvage." That's my mother's great-great-great and a bunch more greats-grandmother.

SHEILA: So, your mother always believed that she was Métis or something?

COYOTE: It was more of a joke. Because I'm darker than most of my family. They would say "there's the *enfant sauvage* again. It shows up every couple of generations."

AISLINN: But that would make you French.

COYOTE: I don't speak French.

AISLINN: Do you speak Algonquin?

COYOTE: I'm not some wannabe. I have an actual ancestor.

AISLINN: Just one, though, from nearly three hundred years ago.

COYOTE: Still counts. *(To SHEILA.)* Still counts, right?

SHEILA: Counts for what?

COYOTE: You know. If I'm Indigenous.

SHEILA: That's not for me to say. That's between you and your community.

AISLINN: Which community are you from?

COYOTE: I told you, that part wasn't recorded. But I'm totally legit. I promise.

          COYOTE, alone, reading from his tablet.

One thousand followers.

PSYCHIC
BELIEVER: Creator bless you, Coyote, and all the work
                 you're doing. These signs are important for
                 all mankind?

NDN
FOLLOWER: I don't care what anyone says, Coyote, I
                 know you're Indigenous. I know you're
                 one of us! Stay out there and keep letting us
                 know what's happening. Don't let—

NEW AGE
BOOKSTORE
OWNER: We are all human. We are all people. We are
                 all Indigenous to this planet. These white
                 buffalo calves are the best hope for—

COYOTE: Ten thousand followers?

DONOR: It's not much but here's five dollars. It's all I
                 have right now. If you can, send video of the
                 calves. I'd give more but—

EAGER
DONOR: Ten bucks a month, my brother! You're onto
                 the truth. I know because a coyote came to
                 me in a dream. Dig that! Never happened
                 before. I'd give more but—

MIRACLE
DONOR: I showed my son the video of the calves and
                 he blinked. For the first time in four months
                 he blinked! He's been in a coma since he
                 crashed his motorcycle. It's a miracle. I'm
                 able to send you a hundred dollars right
                 now and will send more but—

COYOTE: Fifty thousand followers? And yet.

COLIN'S
CLASSMATE: Nice scam you got going, Colin!

COLIN'S
COUSIN: Fuck you, cousin. You better start sharing
               some of this money or we'll tell everyone
               the true story!

PISSED-OFF
ELDER: You act like those buffalo belong to you.
               They belong to the people. They belong to
               the Creator! Even if you're a real Indian,
               that's not how a real Indian acts!

COYOTE: One hundred thousand followers.

TOTAL
NEWBIE: So, okay, total newbie here. I know it's been
               posted before but could someone repost the
               map to the actual Buffalo Pound Lake First
               Nation and not the town of Buffalo Pound
               Lake.

               AISLINN in VANESSA's lab, snooping.
               VANESSA enters. She watches.

VANESSA: Everything is locked up.

               AISLINN isn't startled.

AISLINN: Oh, I know. That's the most prudent thing to
               do. I wouldn't expect anything less from you.

VANESSA: Then what are you doing here?

AISLINN: What did you do with the embryos?

VANESSA: I implanted them.

AISLINN: Not all of them.

VANESSA: Of course not.

AISLINN: No. Of course not. That also wouldn't be
               prudent. Where are they?

VANESSA: Safe.

AISLINN: Oh come on, Vanessa. I'm probably one of the few people around here who actually understands what you're doing.

VANESSA: If I tell you they're safe.

AISLINN: I'm here to ensure that the European Union's investment is secured.

VANESSA: Just the EU's?

AISLINN: It is a considerable amount of money.

VANESSA: I sincerely thank you for it. But it was made crystal clear to me that the research into purifying the herd was the sole focus of your "investment."

AISLINN: Still is. And always will be. You see, though, this is an evolving situation. No one predicted this overreaction to the white calves.

VANESSA: I expected something like this. That's why I wanted to keep it quiet.

AISLINN: It wasn't me who contacted Coyote.

VANESSA: But you're trying to take advantage of his arrival.

AISLINN: Then speak to him and "clear things up."

VANESSA: It's bad enough that he's here with his horror show of wannabes and New Age freaks. We don't need more people disturbing the herd. We don't need more attention.

AISLINN: You're being too cautious. At some point you have to publish your research.

VANESSA:	Publish? Market, you mean.
AISLINN:	Yes, market! Damn it, Vanessa, we are in this to make a euro or two. That was the whole idea, right? Pure bison for the European market.
VANESSA:	I will release this research when I'm ready to release it. Not a day sooner. That's the agreement we have with the EU.
AISLINN:	I know, I know, and I respect that. But this moment, right now, it's a once-in-a-lifetime opportunity.
	(A realization.) Unless…it isn't.
VANESSA:	Isn't what?
AISLINN:	Once in a lifetime. This could happen again, right? Once you map out those calves' genome, this could happen again and again. On purpose. The only question is the scale.
VANESSA:	You want to invite that craziness every time a white bison is born?
AISLINN:	It'll run its course. Once they see these calves aren't connected to the prophecy then we're in the clear.
VANESSA:	You don't understand, this will happen every single time.
AISLINN:	Then we sell tickets. Turn it into a festival. Have bands even. Bison-stock. BisonFest! That's better.
VANESSA:	This is not something to be joking about.
AISLINN:	You don't actually believe in it, do you? The white buffalo thing?

VANESSA:	Why does that matter?
AISLINN:	You're taking it way too seriously. You don't sound like the Vanessa I know.
VANESSA:	We have a connection with the bison. They weren't just a food source for us. It's not something to be taken for granted or messed with. It's a kinship, a responsibility.

SHEILA's house.

SHEILA is working on her sculpture.

AISLINN sips tea.

SHEILA:	God, I'm just not feeling it! Something is blocking me.
AISLINN:	Supposed to be a buffalo?
SHEILA:	You can tell that from this mess?
AISLINN:	Yes. It strongly suggests a buffalo.
SHEILA:	Suggests? Is that all it does?
AISLINN:	I'm not an artist.
SHEILA:	Oh, I don't think I'll ever finish this.
AISLINN:	What's it for?
SHEILA:	I wanted to make a gift for the Elders Lodge.
AISLINN:	I'm sure they'll love it.
SHEILA:	I'm not so sure. They're not exactly into artwork that just "suggests" a buffalo. Bunch a miserable old farts, anyway.
AISLINN:	I don't believe I've heard of Elders described like that.

SHEILA: Oh, no, it's...well, there are some who knew my mother and they always tell me what a wonderful woman she was.

AISLINN: And that's bad, how?

SHEILA: Because, it's their way of asking "What happened to you?" Me, who ran away to be an artist... and came crawling back when I couldn't cut it.

Beat.

You close with your family?

AISLINN: Me? Yes. I suppose. I've never really thought about it. I have two sisters, Siobhan and Roisin, and, well, we're not close-close, but we're civil when we're together. We don't get into any fights at family gatherings. I genuinely like seeing their kids. Their husbands are tolerable.

SHEILA: And your parents?

AISLINN: Divorce used to be illegal in Ireland. If it was legal back then, I'm sure they'd both be alive right now.

SHEILA: They didn't...

AISLINN: Oh no. They were so viciously miserable to each other that they both sought the sweet relief of the grave to escape their marriage.

Pause.

SHEILA: *(Laughing.)* That's not—you shouldn't say things like that.

AISLINN: Always gets a laugh at the pub.

SHEILA: Is that why you're not married?

AISLINN: No, no, no. It's because polygamy is illegal. Too many choices. Pick just one? God kill me if I ever do. You ever marry?

SHEILA: Twice.

AISLINN: And children?

SHEILA: Couldn't.

AISLINN: Oh, I'm sorry. I didn't mean...

SHEILA: It's all right. I had Vanessa and Michael. I didn't miss out.

AISLINN: Well, they turned out great.

SHEILA: Wish I had anything to do with it. Michael, I just had to keep fed and clothed. He was good at school, good at sports, very popular, and had a good head on his shoulders. Never got into any trouble. Well. Not into any kind of trouble that a teenager couldn't get out of. I never had a worry with Michael.

        Pause.

AISLINN: And Vanessa?

SHEILA: I don't know. She's very special, right?

AISLINN: She's extremely intelligent.

SHEILA: She is that. But she has other gifts. When she was little she didn't grieve her parents' death. I was devastated but she acted like it hadn't happened. Michael, he cried for days, but Vanessa didn't even cry. I thought, okay, she's just overwhelmed or in shock, and the grief would come later. It never did. The first anniversary of the car accident was pretty bad for Michael. And for me as well. I could barely get out of bed.

Pause.

Then, I thought I was dreaming, I could smell banana pancakes. But there's Vanessa, in the kitchen, making banana pancakes. She's seven. Standing on a chair by the stove, whipping the batter with her wispy arms.

Sheila sings the first few lines to the chorus of "Escape" by Rupert Holmes.

SHEILA has to recover.

AISLINN: Are you all right?

SHEILA: Vanessa was a seven-year-old version of her mother. That's what Siobhan would do whenever the kids felt bad or I needed cheering up. She would sing to us. That cheesy song, for some reason, always made me feel better. And we all loved Siobhan's banana pancakes. I swear, her parents, especially her mother, is still with her. Never left her. That's why she didn't mourn them.

AISLINN: But she's an atheist.

SHEILA: I know she says that.

AISLINN: I'm pretty sure she believes it too.

It's night.

VANESSA amongst the herd.

She is at peace.

Drums play in the background.

VANESSA: God, people are so noisy.

BABY PETE enters.

BABY PETE:	Hey sis. Is it okay to get closer?
VANESSA:	They know you.
BABY PETE:	Is everything okay? With you, I mean?
VANESSA:	When I'm here, yes.
BABY PETE:	I need to speak to Mom.
VANESSA:	You should've paid more attention when she was talking to us.
BABY PETE:	Is she still talking to you?
VANESSA:	Michael...come on. You still believe that?
BABY PETE:	I'd like to.
VANESSA:	That's not how it works.
BABY PETE:	I need to know what to do if these calves are, you know, the ones.
VANESSA:	If they're the ones, then what happens, happens. There's nothing we can do about it. Prophecies don't care if we're ready or not.
BABY PETE:	Is that you talking, or her?
VANESSA:	Pray about it. Talk to Elders. That's what Aunty would say.
BABY PETE:	I want to know what Mom would say.

Pause.

VANESSA:	Mom believed in the prophecy but I don't think she expected it to be fulfilled in her lifetime. She never spoke about preparing for it.
	(Referring to the bison.) Listen to them. They are our relations. They will tell us. They'll know.

BABY PETE: And what are they saying?

VANESSA: They want you to do something about those stupid people over there. It's keeping them awake.

BABY PETE: We got them away from the fence. They're camping on Bartok's pasture now. Nothing we can do about that. And he's okay with it because they're paying him good.

VANESSA: The noise they're making isn't confined to Bartok's land.

BABY PETE: I'll talk to Coyote again. Get him to set a curfew or something.

VANESSA's lab. Everyone is there.

COYOTE is live-streaming the moment. He has his tablet on the selfie stick.

VANESSA: Coyote, if that thing knocks anything over...

COYOTE: It is a fine-tuned instrument.

VANESSA: Don't make me regret asking you to be here.

AISLINN: Why was that, actually?

VANESSA: The sooner we get this "cleared up" and the message sent to his people, the sooner they bugger off.

BABY PETE: Exciting, isn't it?

VANESSA: It's just going to be an email. Nothing really that dramatic.

SHEILA: Has it arrived yet?

VANESSA: No. We got, maybe, five minutes.

>   *VANESSA taps the refresh button on her computer.*

BABY PETE: Nothing?

VANESSA: Just relax, everyone. It'll be here soon enough.

>   *Pause.*

>   *VANESSA's cell phone rings.*

VANESSA: *(Into phone.)* Yes?... No, not yet—Okay, okay, I'm checking now.

>   *She refreshes her email.*

VANESSA: Okay, everyone. Here it is.

>   *They gather round while she quickly reads it.*

VANESSA: Huh.

BABY PETE: What do you mean, "huh?"

VANESSA: Give me a second.

AISLINN: Are they cattle or bison genes?

>   *VANESSA reads it again. She has to digest this.*

BABY PETE: Come on, sis. What is it?

>   *Pause.*

VANESSA: It's a mutation... We think.

BABY PETE: Think! Can't you guys come up with a straight answer?

VANESSA: It's not in any of the databases that they've searched so far. It still might be a lesser-known gene but...

SHEILA:	But if it isn't?
VANESSA:	These calves are unique. This is the first time we've ever seen this.
BABY PETE:	Like the prophecy says—
VANESSA:	If it holds up to scrutiny.
BABY PETE:	Still.
COYOTE:	They're mutants!
VANESSA:	A mutation does not mean they're mutants. This is a normal occurrence. It's happened throughout the history of evolution. What we don't know is if it was a bovine or bison gene that mutated. And we won't know because we don't have the technology to determine that at this time. We have the genomes for the bovine and most of it for the bison.
BABY PETE:	Well, can you answer this? Did you know this was going to happen?
VANESSA:	Did I know that a mutation was going to happen?
BABY PETE:	Yes.
VANESSA:	No. That's impossible to know. No one could know.
SHEILA:	So, it "just happened."
VANESSA:	It's a one-in-a-billion event!
SHEILA:	We'll have to inform the Elders. There are considerations and protocols that must be followed from now on. My niece admits this is a unique moment. She doesn't want to say that this is a miracle, but I sure am willing to say it.

COYOTE: Even if these buffalo are white because of a mutation?

SHEILA: The prophecy doesn't say how they become white, just that they will be a white buffalo calf.

COYOTE: Then these are the ones?

SHEILA: We'll have to pray on that and consult. Something remarkable has happened here. But now is the time for praying and reflection. I know people are excited but we have to move carefully and with great consideration from now on.

AISLINN: Sounds like someone found their inner Elder.

SHEILA: We all need guidance from the Elders now. Let us do what we have to do.

               AISLINN approaches COYOTE at the camp.

AISLINN: Quite the following you have. Must be a thousand people here. And more are coming. According to the threads on your site.

COYOTE: They all want to witness the miracle. Video feeds aren't doing it for them anymore.

AISLINN: You worry about the damage you're doing to this reserve?

COYOTE: Many of the reserve's people are very welcoming. They like that we're here.

AISLINN: They like the way your people are throwing money around.

COYOTE: Stop calling them "my people."

AISLINN: But they are, Coyote, whether you want to admit it or not. And it's time you showed some leadership. Time for you to tell them to go home. There's nothing to see here.

COYOTE: And yet, you flew in from Ireland.

AISLINN: The EU has a significant investment in this herd.

COYOTE: It's just about money to you.

AISLINN: We are enthusiastically supporting a local, Indigenous economy, and Dr. Brokenhorn's research.

COYOTE: To create white buffalo?

AISLINN: Not white, just, purer.

COYOTE: For the European Union?

AISLINN: Yes. And for the reserve as well.

COYOTE: To do what, exactly?

AISLINN: Eat them! What do you think we were going to do with them? Keep them as pets?

COYOTE: I wouldn't know. You guys have some pretty strange ideas about my people. I've seen those weird Indian amusement parks you have over there.

AISLINN: The European Union is acutely aware of the destructive results of many of its member nations' histories. We are determined to rectify that as much as possible with ethical business practices, such as sourcing our exotic meat products from Indigenous peoples first.

COYOTE: Exotic?

AISLINN: As in, not from Europe.

COYOTE: Just sounds patronizing. "Exotic."

AISLINN: Would you rather we use "foreign"? These bison are foreign to Europe.

COYOTE: What do you mean, "these bison"?

AISLINN: Don't take offence. We have European bison. But they're protected.

COYOTE: So that's why you're buying "these bison"?

AISLINN: That and there really isn't a market for eating Europe's bison. These bison here are part of the story of the "American West." That's what makes them so...

COYOTE: Marketable?

AISLINN: Tasty. Like you said, Europe has restaurant chains and theme parks that embrace North America's Indigenous history, the Wild West and all that. Our customers want the real thing. They want to taste "authenticity."

COYOTE: You want real North American bison killed by real North American "Indians" because you want the taste of the "authentic" Wild West.

AISLINN: Yes. Precisely that.

COYOTE: Would you eat the white ones?

Pause.

AISLINN: That would be something that we need to talk to the First Nation about.

COYOTE: You would eat the white ones!

AISLINN: Well, if this prophecy thing doesn't pan out, why not? They're just bison at that point.

                A moment.

                COYOTE reveals the camera.

COYOTE: *(Smug.)* They're just bison at that point.

BABY PETE: *(Angry thread commenter.)* They're just bison at that point!

SHEILA: *(Angry thread commenter.)* They're just bison at that point?

AISLINN: You're a cunt.

                COYOTE with his selfie stick.

COYOTE: Warriors, this is very hard for me to say but we must respect these sacred animals and move as far away from them as possible. Dr. Brokenhorn says that we're endangering these beautiful animals with our presence and I believe her. I know this is hard because you've seen the many testimonies from our cousins who've travelled to this location. Now, don't get angry with Dr. Brokenhorn. She's only doing what she knows is best for the herd. This is a small place and we are not here to do harm. We are here to do good. We are here to help. I asked the Elders here how we can help and they gave me an answer. This community must truck in their water, paying excessive prices to a white man who is using their bad water to make himself rich. What's sad is that this community sits on top of an aquifer. They have fresh water but they don't have the means to pump it to every house, to ensure that it's always safe to drink, or even a proper sewage system.

Warriors, let us thank the people of Buffalo Pound Lake First Nation for their hospitality. Let us build them a proper water system so they'll never have to rely on the avarice of a white man. Let us give them the ability to properly enjoy their own resource. I know we can do it. I have set up an account page on this site for the water needs of these wonderful people. In the name of the white buffalo. Aho!

> *SFX: Drumming and singing in the distance. Not loud but steady.*

> *AISLINN, BABY PETE walk in on VANESSA at her lab.*

VANESSA: Must you?

BABY PETE: I need you to be honest with me.

VANESSA: I always am.

BABY PETE: Did you do it on purpose?

VANESSA: Augh! Again. What I did on purpose was create a process for making our bison purer. What happened as a result, that I didn't plan on, was that they'd turn out to be white. You can't really plan for mutations.

BABY PETE: Then we need to make some decisions. Fast.

AISLINN: The process you developed, Vanessa, I mean, the splicing, can be patented. In Europe, anyway.

BABY PETE: Okay, now this I don't understand.

AISLINN: The mutation, however it happened, is permanent. If these girls have offspring, odds are good they'll be white as well.

BABY PETE: It'll happen over and over again?

VANESSA: Most likely, if their offspring are females. It's locked into their DNA, which they'll pass on to their descendants.

AISLINN: The demand for white bison would be enormous. With licensing fees, you and the band could become extremely wealthy.

BABY PETE: No.

AISLINN: Look. Your people don't have to do the slaughtering, if you feel that strongly about it. It's the process you've developed that's the most interesting to us. We can take white buffalo embryos/ and grow them—

BABY PETE: Listen to me, Aislinn. No. We will not sell you or anybody the white buffalo, their embryos or whatever slicing thing you mentioned.

AISLINN: We co-own this research. We are your partners.

BABY PETE: The research was for purer buffalo. Not white buffalo.

AISLINN: But they're a result of the work.

BABY PETE: Every single white buffalo is sacred to us, and to many other people.

AISLINN: Every single white buffalo cannot be the sign of the prophecy.

VANESSA: This is why I was hoping it was a bovine gene.

AISLINN: Then call it a subspecies. Like mules.

VANESSA: A mule is a hybrid.

AISLINN: People buy and sell mules all the time because people create them all the time. Mules are great animals.

VANESSA:	I didn't create them for a burger franchise.
AISLINN:	But you did create them for a burger franchise and restaurants and theme parks. With our money. Intended or not, this was why you were purifying the herd.

SHEILA enters.

SHEILA:	Coyote's people are blockading the road. They've set up a checkpoint. They're searching cars for drugs and booze.
BABY PETE:	They're getting out of control.
SHEILA:	Coyote sat in with the band councillors.
BABY PETE:	What? They didn't inform me.
SHEILA:	He asked about what were some of the concerns on the reserve. They said "drugs and booze." Then he asked if he could do anything about it.
BABY PETE:	So, he's doing this with their blessing?
SHEILA:	He is.
AISLINN:	He's trying to take control of the calves.
SHEILA:	Everyone is. And yes, before you say it, it worries me. It worries me plenty. You worry me.
AISLINN:	Excuse me, but I've only had the best interests of the reserve.
SHEILA:	Aislinn, please, show me a little respect.
AISLINN:	Okay, yes, let me rephrase. Our interests are also the same as your interests.
SHEILA:	I'm not sure I know what your interests really are.

AISLINN:	The research and the bison.
SHEILA:	Yes, the research. The buffalo meat. But the calves too? We've had this agreement with you for many years now, but you suddenly show up when the calves are born.
AISLINN:	Even we know they're special.
SHEILA:	Or were they expected?
VANESSA:	No one could have predicted them, Aunty.
SHEILA:	With infinite money and manipulation, something was bound to come up.
AISLINN:	The purest American bison was all we hoped for. And now, some fraud is trying to take them away from you. He plans to bribe your community with your own water.
SHEILA:	Yes, we know. It's all over his website. For someone you think is so devious, he's certainly open about his plans.
AISLINN:	Chief, you can't let the people fall for this.
BABY PETE:	Oh, it's "chief" now.
AISLINN:	Start acting like one.
SHEILA:	Do you know what it's like to not have clean drinking water for twenty years? Michael and every chief before him has been pushing for clean water. They haven't delivered—
BABY PETE:	Aunty, I'm right here.
SHEILA:	I know, nephew, it's not your fault. But waiting for the federal government has got us nowhere.
BABY PETE:	People here will listen to him if he can make the water flow.

VANESSA:	Do you trust him?
BABY PETE:	If he doesn't do it then he's no different than the feds.
AISLINN:	If you accept his proposal, you give him legitimacy. It allows him to flex more of his power.
BABY PETE:	I know. He's got the councillors on his side. He's got many of the Elders too. Who knows how many band members. And that crowd of "pilgrims" that keeps growing every day.
AISLINN:	What about help from other reserves?
BABY PETE:	Yeah, "help." The help they're offering is take them from us to "protect them." Could the EU send some kind of police or security because the feds and province keep blowing me off.

AISLINN shrugs.

	Fuck! We could've spent that land claim money on new houses or a functioning water treatment plant!
VANESSA:	Michael. Don't. You were right about purchasing the herd. I saw the difference they made to us.
SHEILA:	Every morning, there were always Elders praying. Out there in the West Range, no matter the weather. Families, together, watching, just wanting to be near them. It was magical.
VANESSA:	We are them, they are us. If we lose them...
BABY PETE:	We won't lose them.

VANESSA: Don't say that. They were taken from us once before. The only miracle I actually believe in is that they survived at all.

Later, BABY PETE on his phone.

BABY PETE: Tell the minister that I have over people squatting on the only road leading to my reserve and I'm hearing that even more are coming. *(Listens.)* Yes, they're disruptive. We don't have a campground, we barely have enough housing for ourselves. We rely on trucked-in water and they're— *(Listens.)* BisonFest. Who's calling it "BisonFest"! *(Listens.)* It's not a festival and we're not ordering porta-potties. Speaking of, who knows where these people are taking a shit and we've got enough runoff from the— *(Listens.)* This isn't on us! We didn't expect those calves to be born. *(Listens.)* Yes, they're "that big a deal." They're sacred to us. But these clowns out here are causing—*(Listens.)* Well, they're blocking our access to the highway. You couldn't send more police to the Qu'Appelle detachment, could you? *(Listens.)* Blocking! Not blockading! Don't call in—*(Listens.)* No. You don't need to call in the army. Not yet, any—*(Listens.)* No. No army. Cops. We need police.

Outside the band office.

COYOTE confronts AISLINN.

COYOTE: I know it was you who called that reporter from APTN. I'm being called a fake Indian all over the news.

AISLINN: You can't even get the phrase right, it's "pretendian."

COYOTE:	I have followers pulling their donations. Demanding refunds.
AISLINN:	You shouldn't have lied to them.
COYOTE:	That money was going to bring water to this community. It was going to do a lot of good here.
AISLINN:	You made some big promises. Be a shame if you can't deliver.
COYOTE:	I should banish you. That would humble you up quick.
AISLINN:	Banish me? Banish me from where?
COYOTE:	You see that camp over there? There's about a thousand people there. If I ask them to surround you and escort you off this reserve, they will do it.
AISLINN:	You think they'll listen to you after they see that story? After they see your brothers laugh about how you loved to dress up in buckskins as a kid and run around with a tomahawk? The best part was when your sister mimicked your war cry right into the camera.

She silently mimics a Hollywood war cry.

COYOTE:	You can't turn on the tap and take a drink of water here. You can't do anything with it until you boil it. Do you know how much time and energy that takes? Every single day, boiling water. Add that up. Measure that, if you can. It's not just clean water you took from them. You took time away from them. That's on you.

AISLINN:	This community doesn't need anything from your online group of wannabe Indians and fake Métis.
COYOTE:	We have an ancient connection to this land.
AISLINN:	You're all a bunch of fucking colonizers. Just like your ancestors.

VANESSA in the west range along the fence.

COYOTE enters and tries to wave at her.

VANESSA:	I'm busy.
COYOTE:	Can you give me a DNA test?
VANESSA:	You want to know how much bison DNA you have?
COYOTE:	No. Native.
VANESSA:	Native what?
COYOTE:	Native-native. You know, Indigenous. First Nations.
VANESSA:	Why?
COYOTE:	To prove that I'm Indigenous!
VANESSA:	Ahhhhhhhhh. No. I can't.
COYOTE:	Why not?
VANESSA:	It's not possible.
COYOTE:	You do it with the buffalo.
VANESSA:	Prove that they're Indigenous?
COYOTE:	You know what I mean.

VANESSA: Look. I know what's bovine DNA because cattle have been tracked and registered for generations. We have a pretty clear and documented history of every breed in North America. Plus, we have a pretty good bison genome to work with. We can compare and contrast. We don't have that with human beings.

COYOTE: But can't you look for Indigenous DNA?

VANESSA: Indigenous people aren't a different species. There's a point one per cent difference between you and any other person on this planet. The difference between you and a random chimpanzee is less than two per cent. There's no gene that says Cree, Dakota or Algonquin. Besides, I'm a veterinarian.

COYOTE: And a geneticist. You must know someone who can help me? *(Pause.)* Please.

VANESSA: Coyote, I've already explained to you why it will not work for you. But you are a very, very...

COYOTE: There's nothing you can do?

VANESSA: No.

COYOTE: Do you think I'm Indigenous?

VANESSA: Not my problem. I know I'm Cree and Dakota because I know where my ancestors are buried. But I catch shade because I don't speak Dakota or Cree well enough. I got a university education. I don't do ceremony.

COYOTE: What do you say to them?

VANESSA: Not my problem. But you are my problem.

COYOTE: How so?

VANESSA:	Your people.
COYOTE:	They're not my people.
VANESSA:	Fine. Whatever you want to call them. Those campers who are here because of you, they need to go.
COYOTE:	I've suggested they not gather here but I can't tell them where to go. And none of them want to miss whatever's going to happen.
VANESSA:	What do you think is going to happen?
COYOTE:	The world will be healed. It won't be so fucked-up, and polluted, and violent anymore. People will embrace each other as a global family. There will finally be peace. There will finally be happiness.
VANESSA:	You really believe that?
COYOTE:	Everyone here does. That's why we're here. I know you think we're inconvenient but we're good people. We really want the world to be good for everyone, no matter who they are.
VANESSA:	Look, if you really, really want to know what the prophecy says, speak to an Elder. A real Elder. Listen carefully. Don't interrupt. You might learn something that you didn't expect.
COYOTE:	And the DNA test?
VANESSA:	There is no test.

VANESSA exits.

SHEILA and her sculpture. It's two very life-like white buffalo calves.

She stares at them.

They seem to glow.

SHEILA: We are buffalo people. I am a buffalo woman.

SHEILA becomes a buffalo.

AISLINN, BABY PETE and COYOTE join her and become the herd.

SHEILA: Someone is praying.

BABY PETE: But the words are wrong.

AISLINN: Tobacco is burning.

COYOTE: But the medicine is wrong.

SHEILA: Sparks from the smudge catch the grass.

BABY PETE: A fire.

AISLINN: A fire.

COYOTE: A fire!

ALL
TOGETHER: Fire!

SHEILA: We move the calves away.

BABY PETE: We run to the valley.

AISLINN: We run to the water.

COYOTE: A bull turns and runs back.

SHEILA: He charges the shack.

BABY PETE: "Fire!" I shout. And ram the shack again. "Fire!"

AISLINN: Our cousin runs out. She sees the fire approaching.

BABY PETE: Fire!

COYOTE:	Run!
AISLINN:	She runs.
SHEILA:	She is safe.

We see VANESSA watch the lab burn.

A commotion as the herd now becomes the community and the campers trying to put the fire out with shovels, blankets, even their feet.

The lab is lost but the fire is out.

VANESSA stares at the smoking ruin of her lab.

It is evening. The stars are out. It is warm.

Everyone is still there.

AISLINN: *(To VANESSA.)* The embryos. The research.

SFX: Uneasy quiet builds to a rowdy noise.

SFX: Drums start up.

VANESSA: *(To COYOTE.)* Tell them to be quiet!

COYOTE raises his hand for quiet.

The drums quickly quiet down.

BABY PETE: It was a couple of our youth. Performing a ceremony for these wannabes here.

SHEILA: A ceremony?

BABY PETE: A genuine, Indian, buffalo-cleansing ceremony. At a hundred dollars a person.

AISLINN: Bet you they would've paid a thousand.

BABY PETE: Aislinn, please.

AISLINN: Just saying.

SHEILA: It didn't need to be said.

COYOTE: *(To the crowd, and into selfie stick.)* Warriors! We had been graciously invited by this community and now we must—

VANESSA: Your people have done enough, Coyote!

COYOTE: We helped put it out.

VANESSA: Is this the peace and harmony you were looking for? Is this one of the signs?

>   *VANESSA reveals a small white box. She opens it and holds up a pair of small plastic tubes. They are the last two remaining embryos.*

AISLINN: What are you doing? Those should be refrigerated.

VANESSA: People, listen to me. What I am holding is the future of these white bison. They are worth millions to the European partners and to our reserve.

>   *The buffalo make themselves known. We see shadows of the Cree and Dakota ancestors.*

COYOTE: Everyone is silent.

BABY PETE: Even the wind holds its breath.

AISLINN: The buffalo surround the crowd.

SHEILA: I swear I can see our ancestors, watching us. Their hands clutching their throats.

VANESSA: All my knowledge, all my work, all my dreams have been poured into these two vials. These are identical to the girls that were born. These are white buffalo.

SHEILA:	My niece. What are you thinking?
VANESSA:	*(Referring to the bison.)* I'm thinking they know better than me.
COYOTE:	Are those clones?
VANESSA:	These are the purest bison on this reserve. And they are white.

She puts them back into the box.

Who should I give them to?

SHEILA:	We can't answer that.
VANESSA:	Then who can?
AISLINN:	Tell me you backed them up. You still have backups, yes? Please tell me you have backups.
VANESSA:	This was never my home, you know. I never fit in.
SHEILA:	You're not talking sense.
VANESSA:	I was always the strange one. The weirdo. The one who can never forget. I couldn't wait to leave this place when I was old enough. But I missed it. And when I had the chance to work with the bison, here, it was my ancestors feeling the rumble of the bison stampeding to them.
AISLINN:	Vanessa, please, where are your backups?
VANESSA:	In there.

She points to the smoking ruin of her lab.

She hands the box to SHEILA.

VANESSA: You decide.

                  She walks away.

VANESSA: I have one more thing to do. For your own safety, I suggest you all stay here.

                  VANESSA is at the gate.

                  SFX: A quiet prairie night.

                  She stares at the herd.

You are the millions. Each of you has a story. You have a dream. This land is open. Take back your land. Be free!

                  She opens the gate.

                  She stomps, she chuffs, she calls the buffalo to her.

                  SFX: The herd runs towards her.

                  The sound increases, the ground shakes.

                  She is consumed by a bright, white light.

                  She disappears.

                  We see the night sky.

                  A star falls.

                  Blackout.

                  The end.

The Herd Study Guide

Excerpted from the Resource Guide for The Herd *developed by Citadel Theatre. Reproduced by permission of Citadel Theatre.*

Themes in *The Herd*

Science vs. Spirituality

> "Every single white buffalo cannot be the sign of the prophecy."
>
> –Aislinn, *The Herd*

Is the birth of the white twin bison calves the fulfillment of a prophecy, or is it a feat of modern science? This is the primary conflict in the play, *The Herd,* and the question that all of the characters are trying to answer. But to better understand the tension between science and spirituality, it is a good idea to first look at each theme separately.

Themes and characters associated with science began to appear in art as early as the Renaissance and Baroque periods. It became increasingly popular to include characters that were doctors, chemists, and surgeons in literary and theatrical work, and these characters were often used to add realism or credibility to concepts explored in fiction. As science and technological innovation progressed rapidly in the early 19th century and the notion of Enlightenment became more widespread, discussions of mathematics and science became more prevalent too. As a theme, science can represent modernity, innovation, and logic. In fiction, science is also often used to ask questions about morality. Think about *Frankenstein* (1818) by Mary Shelley, in which Dr. Frankenstein's monster turns against its creator. This is a classic example of the concept of science being used in art to show us that technological innovation may come at a moral cost—and it asks the reader to consider the ethical implication of humans having too much power over nature. In *The Herd,* Dr. Vanessa Brokenhorn, the veterinarian and animal geneticist, is the character that represents the scientific perspective. She is objective, analytical, and deeply considerate of the moral implications of her scientific work.

Spirituality can be related to religion, but it is something entirely separate. Spirituality has more to do with the belief that there is something greater than "the self," and that there is something beyond the human sensory experience that is cosmic or divine in nature. As a theme, spirituality has pretty much always been a preoccupation for humans and appears in many of our earliest records or art and the written word. It also involves the exploration of universal themes like love, compassion, altruism, life after death, wisdom, and truth.

In *The Herd*, many characters are hoping to find more spirituality in their lives, but few actually do. Vanessa's older brother, "Baby Pete," is the Chief of the Buffalo Pound Lake First Nations, and he is one of the strongest believers in the prophecy of the White Buffalo Calf Woman. He—like many other characters in the story—believe that the birth of twin white bison is a sign that there will be unity and peace between all people, and that prosperity is coming. Though Baby Pete believes in the prophecy, he is often shown looking to others throughout the narrative, suggesting that he is still not secure in his own personal and spiritual beliefs.

Similarly, the character Coyote Jackson is fascinated by spirituality, but he seems to only be interested in it on a surface level. As an internet influencer, he interacts more with the prophecy as a way to further his own career, even if deep down his motivation may be to solidify his own identity.

Sheila Kennedy, Vanessa and Baby Pete's aunt, is probably the most spiritual character in the story, but even she feels a "disconnect" or a "block" that she often refers to. While her community has labelled her as an Elder, she is resistant to fully taking on this role. She often communicates with her sister, Siobhan, who has passed away. Though she is hesitant to take on her new role as a leader, Sheila does seem to have access to and knowledge of the spiritual realm in a way that no other character in the play does. After witnessing the miracle of the white bison, she says to her community, "Something remarkable has happened here. But now is the time for praying and reflection.

I know people are excited, but we have to move carefully and with great consideration from now on." This emphasizes that Sheila has the ability to consider the moral and spiritual implications of what is happening in their community, and that she truly believes in a power that is greater than herself and looks to it for guidance.

The tensions between science, modernity, social media, and spirituality are what drive the characters in *The Herd*. The narrative shows that just because a character believes in spirituality, it doesn't mean that they live a spiritual life. In fact, Vanessa, the very embodiment of science, may be the character in the end who is most concerned with the spiritual implications of her scientific discovery.

Reflection Question:

Do you think that *The Herd* separates science and spirituality, or do you think it shows how they can co-exist?

Identity

> "They're NOT my people."
> –Coyote Jackson, *The Herd*

Identity is one of the most common themes in literature and art, and this is likely because the question "Who am I?" is an existential dilemma that all people have to face as they transition from childhood to adulthood. In *The Herd*, Coyote Jackson is the character who has the least stable sense of self. Many times throughout the play, other characters (but mainly Vanessa), refer to the hordes of followers that Coyote has from his internet platform as "his people," to which he always replies "they're NOT my people." To a viewer this is interesting because we witness Coyote pouring all of his energy into communicating with his followers. So if he doesn't see this community as his, how does he actually view them, and why are they so important to him?

Quite early on, we hear voices of internet trolls saying that Coyote is just a white boy from Etobicoke, Ontario, named Colin Jackson, who only has a dubious connection to Indigenous heritage.

This conflicts with the radical image of the "Indigenizer of the Internet" that he markets himself as, and creates a lot of tension between him and other characters like Vanessa and Aislinn. This disconnect between how Coyote sees himself and who he actually is starts to weigh on him more and more throughout the narrative, and in the end, he asks Vanessa if she can do a DNA test to prove his Indigeneity. To this, Vanessa replies, "Indigenous people aren't a different species. There's a point one per cent difference between you and any other person on this planet. The difference between you and a random chimpanzee is less than two per cent. There's no gene that says 'Cree' 'Dakota' or 'Algonquin.'"

This answer is not what Coyote wants to hear, as he is looking for concrete proof of who he is and where he belongs. Vanessa tells him that science can't give him a clean-cut answer, and that if he wants to learn anything he should go speak with an Elder, and really listen to what they have to say.

Reflection Question:

Which themes stood out most to you after watching *The Herd?*

Ownership

> "AISLINN: [Coyote is] trying to take control of the calves.
> SHEILA: Everyone is. And yes, before you say it, it worries me. It worries me plenty. You worry me."
>
> —*The Herd*

As a theme, ownership is related to control, autonomy, and power. A main conflict in *The Herd* is who owns the twin white bison who were born on the Buffalo Pound Lake First Nation? Is it the local Indigenous community who have a spiritual investment in their birth? Is it Dr. Brokenhorn, who made them in a laboratory, and who has sworn to protect the herd? Is it Aislinn and the European Union, who have funded Dr. Brokenhorn's research? Or is it Coyote and the media who want to publicize and commodify this miracle? And can, and should, anyone have ownership over something natural, like an animal?

These questions are complicated, and the play doesn't give us any straight answers. However, *The Herd* does suggest that the history of colonization is actually where this dilemma of ownership started. The notion of "private property" did not exist in this region prior to the arrival of European colonists, who stole the land that was inhabited by the Indigenous Populations and gave it monetary value. To achieve this, the colonizers tried to eradicate the First Nations People and their cultures, and entered into unjust treaties with them that forced them onto reservations. At one point in the narrative, Coyote asks why there is another town on Google Maps called Buffalo Pound Lake, to which Baby Pete replies, "We were supposed to be there when our chief was told to pick a reserve. But the land was 'too good' for Indians so the government shifted us here to be 'near our own kind.' We kept the name as a reminder of where we're supposed to be."

At the play's climax, we see the destruction that has been caused by outside influences when Vanessa's laboratory burns down. At this point, she is forced to decide whether or not it is ethical for someone to own the white bison genome, and if so, who should it belong to?

Reflection Questions:

Do you think that the play, *The Herd*, answers who should have ownership over the white bison? How do you think the playwright, Kenneth T. Williams, complicates the idea of ownership with this story?

History and Context

The Spiritual Significance of White Bison

The legend of the White Buffalo Calf Woman has been told many times across North American Indigenous cultures for the past two thousand years. Although there are different versions of this legend, they all tell a similar story. The People of the Plains in the Lakota Nation (in the South Dakota region) suffered from starvation and disease, so they sent two scouts to search for food. The scouts saw a figure in the distance, and as it approached they realized that it was a beautiful woman dressed in all white. They brought her to their camp, and she gifted their people with a sacred pipe that showed how all things were connected. She spoke of the Seven Sacred Rites, and then said that one day she would return. The maiden turned into a black bison, then a red-brown bison, then a yellow bison, and finally into a white bison. The white bison disappeared into the clouds, and soon after, boundless herds of bison appeared outside their camp—ending the famine and leading the Lakota Nation into a new age of prosperity.

This legend teaches that the food and materials that bison provide are essential and sacred. Indigenous Peoples have always had a deep respect for the natural world around them, and an understanding of the wildlife in the regions that they inhabit. When hunting bison, they would often stampede them over a cliff, which were called buffalo jumps. Every part of the bison was used, which provided their communities with a primary food source as well as materials for clothing, shelter, and tools. Many Elders also interpret the legend of the White Buffalo Calf Woman as a call to respect the women in their communities, and as a reminder to look to them for wisdom and guidance.

Today, the rare birth of a white bison is still considered to be culturally and spiritually significant for Indigenous Peoples. Shannon Kraichy, an education co-ordinator at the Assiniboine Park Zoo who is Métis-Anishinaabe, explains how her elders have taught her the sacred significance of the white bison. "It connects our prayers and our thoughts to the creator and it brings us together as a community," she said. The Assiniboine Park Zoo, in Winnipeg has been a home to the white bison, Blizzard, since he arrived on March 6, 2006 in a snowstorm. Blizzard was born in June of 2005 in a large herd of Plains Bison from Custer State Park, South Dakota. Upon Blizzard's arrival to the zoo, First Nations Elders from the area came forward to explain the spiritual significance of this event, and to ensure that proper protocol would be followed to show respect to this sacred animal. A few Elders held a welcoming ceremony for Blizzard where they smudged him with sweetgrass and sang prayers to the beat of a drum. Dr. Robert E. Wrigley, who was the zoo's curator at the time, described how the calf "stood reverently for the entire performance, as if he knew that he was being honored."

Hundreds of visitors come every year to pay Blizzard their respects. The zoo now has an offering bowl near the bison enclosure, where visitors can leave spiritual offerings like tobacco, sweet grass, sage and cedar. The sign by the bowl reads, "An offering is a respectful way of asking for assistance and is open to anyone. An offering must be made with good energy and good intentions." When asked why so many people come to visit Blizzard, Shannon Kraichy explained that, "They just have such a connection to him and because he is sacred, and he is ceremonial. I know that it is a very personal, spiritual thing between [the people and the bison.]"

While Blizzard isn't the only white bison that has been born in North America over the past 200 years, he is one of very few. In the play, *The Herd*, the characters often refer to the birth of the white bison as a prophecy. This is because many Indigenous communities believe that one day the White Buffalo Calf Woman will return to them in the form of a white bison, and that she will bring unity to all people.

"The arrival of the white buffalo is like the second coming of Christ. It will bring about purity of mind, body, and spirit and unify all nations—black, red, yellow, and white."—Floyd Hand Looks For Buffalo, an Oglala Medicine Man from Pine Ridge, South Dakota.

The Scientific Significance of White Bison

Albinism is the cause of a white animal being born in many species, and sometimes this is the case for bison. The chance of an animal being born with albinism is anywhere from one in 20,000 to one in one million. These bison will remain white throughout their entire lives and may have hearing or vision problems. However, in bison there is another recessive gene from a distant ancestor that causes their fur to turn snow-white, but in this case as they continue to mature they will likely turn brown within a couple of years. This gene is so rare that the chances of it being passed down are one in every 10 million births. The final way that a bison could be born with white fur is if it is a beefalo (or a bison and cattle crossbreed), as Dr. Brokenhorn mentions in the play. In this case the animal would have inherited their white colour from their cattle ancestry. When a white bison is born, an animal geneticist (like Dr. Vanessa Brokenhorn in *The Herd*) might test the animal's genome to see if the cause is albinism, cattle ancestry, or the rare recessive gene. Vanessa's discovery is so scientifically significant because she may have found the genome for this recessive gene, and if the twin bison's fur stays white throughout their entire lives, this would be an extremely rare occurrence.

The decimation of the bison population across North America in the 19th century was initially thought to have eradicated this rare occurrence, but luckily there are still white bison that have been born over the last century who have this recessive gene.

Take a look at this passage from the Assiniboine Park Zoo's website to understand the drastic decline in the bison population over the past 200 years:

"As many as 40 million bison once ranged throughout much of North America. By the late 19th century, following the arrival of colonial Europeans, bison populations were driven nearly to extinction. Overhunting of bison went beyond the economic considerations of the fur trade with federal officials actually advocating for the widespread eradication of the species as a way to force Indigenous communities into the government's reservation system and open up additional land for colonial settlement.

"While reintroduction and breeding efforts have avoided complete extinction of the species, only a fraction of these once huge herds remain. Population fragmentation and loss of prairie habitat present ongoing challenges for the conservation of the species in the wild."—Assiniboine Park Zoo, Winnipeg Manitoba

In *The Herd*, Vanessa claims to have accidentally bred twin white bison while she is trying to "purify" their genetic makeup so that they will be closer to their ancestors. Since she does this in a laboratory setting, it creates a huge media frenzy, and garners significant interest from her investors at the European Union. Aislinn (from the EU) tells Vanessa that if she has the genome for the white bison, she could get it patented in Europe and start a selective breeding process. She even goes on to envision a world where they could mass-produce white bison and create a brand, festivals, and could sell their meat for a high price.

In Canada, genes can still be patented—in other words, those who claim to have first identified a gene can apply to have exclusive rights to that specific sequence of DNA. Once someone is granted a gene patent, they can dictate how the gene is used in both commercial settings (such as clinical genetic testing) and non-commercial settings (such as laboratory research), for twenty years. This means that companies often have sole ownership over genetic testing of any genes that they have patented. While the supreme courts in many countries like the United States and Australia have made it illegal to patent human genes in recent years, it is still legal to do this in Canada. Additionally, in most countries individuals and organizations are still able to patent genes for animals and other living organisms.

The question is, should people be allowed to own a specific sequence of DNA? The more that genetic research advances, the more we need to consider the ethics behind it. What should scientists, like Dr. Brokenhorn, use their discoveries for?

Reflection Questions:

Does the play *The Herd* remind you of any other stories that you have heard of in the news? Why do you think the playwright, Kenneth T. Wiliams, incorporated science into a story about spirituality?

Social Media

In the play, Aislinn clashes with the character Coyote Jackson, who refers to himself as an "Indigenizer of the Internet." This social media star uses his influence to get hundreds of people to come to the Buffalo Pound Lake First Nation to witness the prophecy of the white bison come true. While Coyote criticizes Aislinn for her commodification of Indigenous Culture for profit, she accuses him of doing the same thing with his social media following.

Over the past few decades, social media has exploded, and using it is now engrained in our culture. According to researchers at Maryville University, "the evolution of social media has been fueled by the human impulse to communicate and by advances in digital technology." They define social media as any form of electronic communication through which users create online communities to share information. In 2005, a year after Facebook was launched to the public, the PEW Research Center reported that 5% of American adults used social media. By 2019, that number jumped to 72%. But while social media might have developed from a desire to communicate, it has also become an essential tool for marketing. With the rise of social media came the rise of the "influencer." According to the Digital Marketing Institute, that is "someone who has established credibility in a specific industry, has access to a huge audience and can persuade others to act based on their recommendations." While many influencers are seen as trustworthy sources, the reality is that they are still being paid by companies to market products to their followers. Influencers are also their own brand and can use ideologies and political activism to advance their own careers.

The playwright, Kenneth T. Williams, invites the audience to question Coyote's motives. We see how his followers' presence is destructive to the community and nature around them, even when they are trying to help. Coyote tries to educate others about Indigenous culture, and even tries to raise funds for the Buffalo Pound Lake First Nation so that they can get clean drinking water, but he is still operating under a system that has done so much damage to Indigenous communities and their land. In a way, Williams is holding up a mirror to modern society and asking if online political activism is effective, or if it is just another form of commercialization for profit.

Reflection Questions:

What are the parallels in *The Herd* between Coyote Jackson and his followers, and Aislinn and the European Union? Do you think that either group is actually interested in protecting the white bison and the Indigenous community at Buffalo Pound Lake?

Glossary

Albinism:

A group of genetic conditions marked by little or none of the pigment melanin in the skin, hair, and/or eyes. People or animals with albinism may have vision problems and white or yellow hair; reddish, violet, blue or brown eyes; and pale skin, fur, or coat.

Buffalo jumps:

A buffalo jump is a cliff formation which the Indigenous People of North America historically used to hunt and kill Plains bison in mass quantities.

Capitalism:

Capitalism was invented by the 18th-century philosopher Adam Smith, who is credited as being the "father of modern economics." It is an economic and political system in which a country's trade and industry are controlled by private owners for profit rather than by the state.

Commercialization:

Commercialization refers to the introduction of a new product or production method into the market for consumption.

Geneticist:

A geneticist is a biologist who studies genetics, the science of genes, heredity, and variation of organisms.

Genome:	In biology, it is the complete set of genes or genetic material present in a cell or organism.
Globalization:	Globalization is the connection of different parts of the world. Globalization results in the expansion of international cultural, economic, and political activities.
Patented:	A patent is a legal right to an invention or research discovery given to a person or entity without interference from others who wish to replicate, use, or sell it.
Selective breeding:	Selective breeding involves choosing parents with particular characteristics to breed together and produce offspring with more desirable characteristics. Humans have selectively bred plants and animals for thousands of years, including crop plants with better yields.